The Very Stinky Fly Hunt

To my newest nephew, Noah
– AW

A catalogue record for this book is available from the National Library of Australia

ISBN: 9781486318780 (hbk)
ISBN: 9781486321605 (pbk)
ISBN: 9781486318797 (epdf)
ISBN: 9781486318803 (epub)

Published by:
CSIRO Publishing
36 Gardiner Road, Clayton VIC 3168
Private Bag 10, Clayton South VIC 3169
Australia

Telephone: +61 3 9545 8400
Email: publishing.sales@csiro.au
Website: www.publish.csiro.au
Sign up to our email alerts: publish.csiro.au/earlyalert

Edited by Dr Kath Kovac
Cover, text design and layout by Cath Pirret Design
Printed by Ingram Lightning Source

CSIRO acknowledges the Traditional Owners of the lands that we live and work on across Australia and pays its respect to Elders past and present. CSIRO recognises that Aboriginal and Torres Strait Islander peoples have made and will continue to make extraordinary contributions to all aspects of Australian life including culture, economy and science. The use of Western science in this publication should not be interpreted as diminishing the knowledge of plants, animals and environment from Indigenous ecological knowledge systems.

Note for readers: A glossary can be found at the back of the book.

Note for teachers: Teacher notes are available at: https://www.publish.csiro.au/book/8180/#forteachers

Jun25_RP_ILS

The Very Stinky Fly Hunt

Andrea Wild

ILLUSTRATED BY
Karen Erasmus

CSIRO PUBLISHING

Keith is a fly hunter.

No, a fly hunter.

But why does Keith hunt flies?

Why not swish them, swat them,
squish them or squash them?

Because he loves them!

Keith loves flies because they are important to nature.
They pollinate flowers and clean up waste.

He loves them so much that he knows all their names:
from *Achias australis* to *Zinza grandis*.

Keith is so in love with flies, he made hunting them his job.
He is a dipterist – a fly-loving scientist!

Keith knows how to catch flies. He chases
them with long nets.

He sets up special traps. He takes the flies back to his lab to study.

Keith has lots of questions buzzing around his mind. How many species of flies are there? Where do they live? And where do they fit in the fly family tree?

But there's one fly Keith can't seem to catch. *Clisa australis* is missing.

Clisa australis once lived in bat caves, where their babies
had plenty to eat – bat poo for breakfast, lunch and dinner.

But no one has seen this poo-loving fly for a very long time.
Is the species extinct?

Keith visits the bat caves to search for the fly.

But the entrance is blocked and he can't get in.

Where else could he look for them?
Where else could a fly that loves poo hide?

I think I can guess – how about you?

A pit toilet in a
national park is
the perfect place!

Keith begins his
very stinky fly hunt.

He hunts on weekdays.

He hunts on weekends.

He even hunts on holidays.

But he still doesn't catch this rare and hard to find fly.

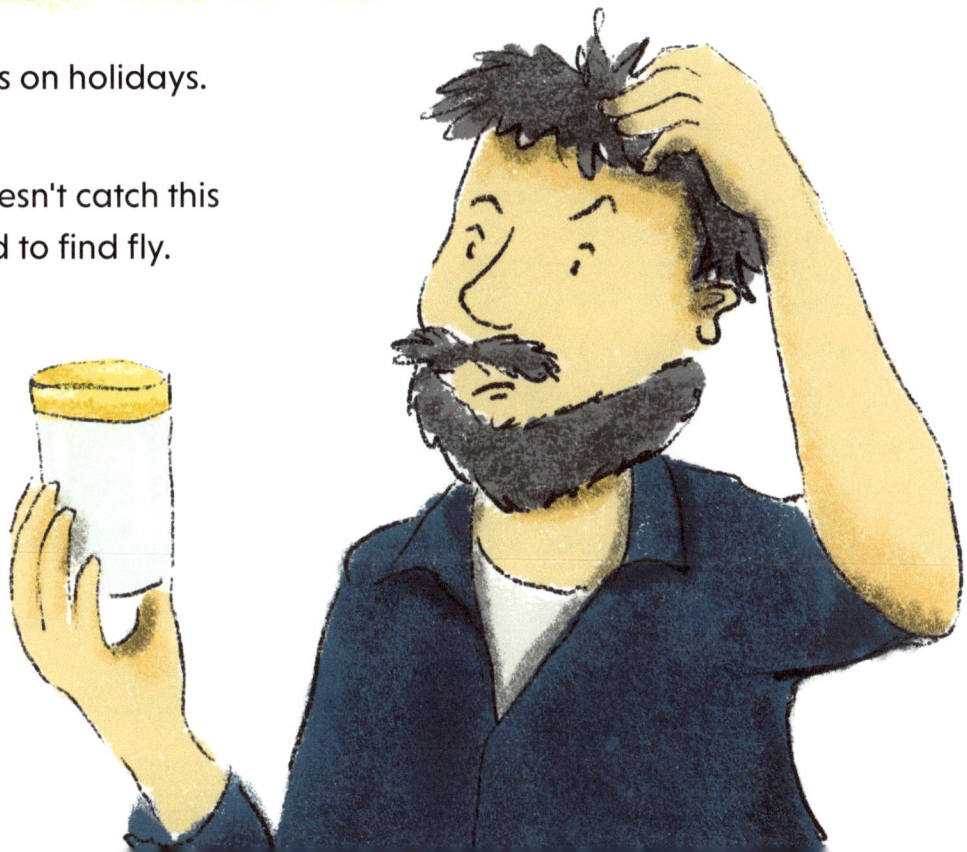

Keith has tried toilet after toilet with no luck.

But a fly hunter's work is never done. Apart from *Clisa australis*, there are zillions of different species to study.

One day Keith sets up a tent-like trap to find out
which species of flies live in a patch of rainforest.

And can you believe it? *Clisa australis* flies right in!

Woo-hoo!

Keith has finally caught this very special fly to study in his lab.

But he doesn't want to give up his very stinky fly hunt.

Since he has found one *Clisa australis* fly, could there be more?

Keith decides to visit the beach.

But he doesn't build sandcastles.

He doesn't surf waves.
He doesn't even try to spot whales.

You guessed it. He goes to the toilet to hunt for flies.

Surprise!

Keith is amazed to find a whole party of flies!

And these flies seem to be dancing.
What do their moves mean?

They also look a little different from *Clisa australis*. Could they be a new species?

Keith now has more questions buzzing around his mind. But that's exciting, because it's something new to discover!

If flies aren't your thing,

you could search for sharks
or birds or fungi or flowers.

Nature holds so much for you to discover.

Keith loves hunting flies.
So for him,

the very stinky fly hunt continues.

Dr Keith Bayless, the fly hunter

Keith studied entomology and genetics at university, and then did a PhD in entomology. He is now a dipterist at CSIRO's Australian National Insect Collection in Canberra.

The Australian National Insect Collection is like a library of insects! Scientists around the world can borrow and study more than 12 million specimens: flies disguised as bees, tiny wasps that look like tea leaves, butterflies as big as birds and many more. The collection reveals what insects live where in Australia, and shows how this has changed over time.

Keith's job at the insect collection is to study Australia's flies. Although our country has 25,000 fly species, fewer than 7,000 species have been given a scientific name. We know almost nothing about the rest! Where do they live? How are they related to each other? Are they becoming extinct? Keith is trying to find out!

'Australia's flies are very diverse and very important to nature,' he says. 'They pollinate flowers, helping plants make seeds. They recycle waste like poo, dead animals and dead plants, helping create new soil.'

'There is so much more we need to find out about Australia's flies and their roles in nature. Some flies are pesky and some are stinky, but they are all amazing. Even the smallest creatures matter.'

Searching for Clisa australis

Many species of flies eat poo. The fly species that stars in this story was given its scientific name, *Clisa australis*, in 1966 by a dipterist named David McAlpine. David found the species living in caves in Carrai National Park in north-east New South Wales. The flies' babies (called larvae or maggots) were feeding on the poo of bent-wing bats that also lived in the caves.

After *Clisa australis* was named, scientists spotted it a few more times around New South Wales. Then it went missing for more than 30 years. Had it become extinct? Keith wanted to find out – and pit toilets were the perfect place to look. Just like caves, they are dark, humid and full of poo!

Pit toilets don't use water to flush away poo. And they don't use chemicals, which kill insects such as flies. Instead, the poo just falls into a deep pit, where insects and fungi break it down into soil. Plus, pit toilets are easier to visit than caves. You don't need special equipment to enter them, and they are often located in national parks that are easy to get to.

Luckily for Keith, his fly hunt wasn't as stinky as it could have been. National parks are beautiful places to visit, and he only had to look for adult flies on the toilet walls, not look for maggots in the poo!

Keith's very stinky fly hunt continues. Were the flies he saw dancing *Clisa australis*, or were they a new species? The fly's closest relatives live far away on Lord Howe Island and in South-East Asia. They are related to fruit flies, even though they don't eat fruit. What does the family tree of these related species look like? And how many other related species are there?

Every answer leads to new, exciting questions. Science never stops!

Glossary

Dipterist – a scientist who studies flies (insects in the group known as Diptera)

Diverse – showing a lot of variety

Entomology – the study of insects

Extinct – when a species no longer exists anywhere on Earth

Family tree – a diagram showing the relationships between different living things

Pollinate – transfer pollen from male to female flower parts so seeds can develop

Scientific name – a unique name given to a species as part of the international system of naming

Species – a unique group of living things that share similar features and can breed with each other to produce young that can also successfully breed

A dipterist's equipment

Malaise trap – a tent-like trap that catches flying insects and funnels them into a bottle

Microscope – for looking at the tiny details of amazing flies

Net – for catching flies while chasing them around the bush

Yellow pans – simple plastic pans used to attract flying insects that like yellow flowers

Acknowledgements

This book was written on the traditional lands of the Ngunnawal People in Canberra, Australia.

It is dedicated to the scientists who work at the Australian National Insect Collection at CSIRO and to all children who dream of becoming scientists.

Thank you to Dr Keith Bayless for sharing this true story.

Thank you to my editors, Melinda Chandler and Mark Hamilton.

www.ingramcontent.com/pod-product-compliance
Lightning Source LLC
Chambersburg PA
CBHW042011080426

42734CB00002B/51